What colour?

Lucy und Fred sind bei ihrer Oma zu Besuch. Sie wohnt in einem großen, alten Haus, in dem es viel zu entdecken gibt. Sie gehen auf den Dachboden und finden eine große Kiste, **a big box.** Hier kannst du sehen, was sie alles finden.

Suche alle Gegenstände oben im Bild und male sie in den richtigen Farben an.

The spider is black.
The knife is grey and black.
The flag of Germany is black, red and yellow.
The teddy is brown.
The shoes are blue.
The bats are black.
The socks are green.
The gold is gold.
The skis are pink.
The book is red.

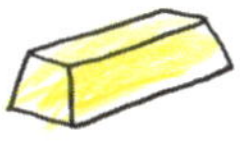

At home
Zu Hause

Lösung

Hello! My name is ...

Stell dich vor!

Lösung

Du kannst so einen Steckbrief auf Englisch von dir schreiben. Zeige ihn deinen Eltern und Freunden.

This is me

Male hier ein Bild von dir selbst hin oder klebe ein Foto ein.

Schreibe jetzt drei Sätze auf Englisch auf, die dich beschreiben. Benutze dabei die Wörter in den folgenden Listen. Nehme für jeden Satz ein Wort aus jeder Zeile. So könnte zum Beispiel dein erster Satz lauten:

My hair is long. – Meine Haare sind lang.

My	eyes	are	long
My partner's	hair	is	short
Her	mouth		blue
	teeth		brown
	skin		blond
	name		green
	years		red
			black
			white

1. My hair is short
2. My eyes is brown
3. My mouth is Normal

a

She lives in

Lösung

Wie siehst du aus?

Wörter, die du nicht kennst, schlägst du im Wörterbuch nach. Schwierige Wörter kannst du noch einmal aufschreiben.

The family

A. Verbinde jeweils das richtige englische Wort mit dem deutschen Wort.

mum	Schwester
brother	Oma
grandma	Mama
dad	Bruder
granddad	Opa
sister	Papa

B. **This is Lucy's family.** Das ist Lucys Familie. Trage die Namen der Familienmitglieder in die Kästchen.

At home
Zu Hause

Lösung

A. mum – Mama, brother – Bruder, grandma – Oma, dad – Papa, grandad – Opa, sister – Schwester

B. im Uhrzeigersinn von oben links:
dad, mum, sister, brother

My clothes

Wo trägt man diese Kleidungsstücke? Ergänze die Körperteile in den Sätzen.

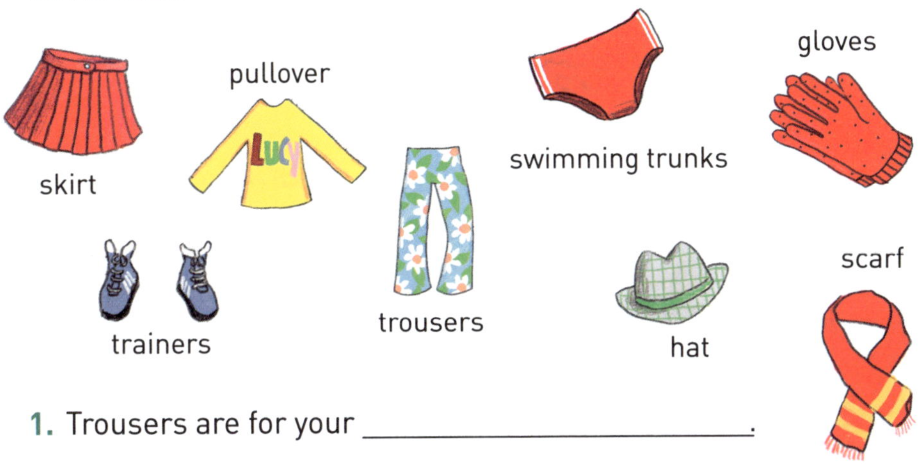

1. Trousers are for your ____________________.
2. Trainers are for your ____________________.
3. A pullover is for your ____________ and ____________.
4. A hat is for your ____________________.
5. A scarf is for your ____________________.
6. Gloves are for your ____________________.
7. Swimming trunks are for your ____________________.
8. A skirt is for your ____________________.

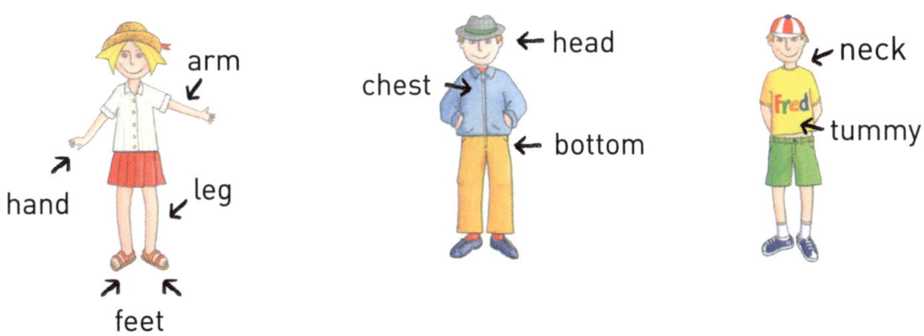

Lösung

1. legs
2. feet
3. chest and arms
4. head
5. neck
6. hands
7. bottom
8. bottom and legs

Lucy and Fred

Ergänze die Sätze mit **is** oder **are**.

1. Lucy's hair ___is___ blond.
2. Fred's shoes ___~~Is~~ are___ blue.
3. Lucy's sandals ___are___ red.
4. Fred's T-shirt ___is___ short.
5. Lucy's skirt ___is___ red.
6. Fred's shorts ___is___ green.
7. Lucy's shirt ___is___ white.
8. Fred's hair ___are___ short.

Lösung

1. is
2. are
3. are
4. is
5. is
6. are
7. is
8. is

Do you know these animals?

Kreuze die Tiere an, die du schon auf Englisch benennen kannst.

Wie viele Tiere sind es? Schreibe die Zahl in das Kästchen. Kannst du die Zahlen und Tiere auf Englisch sagen? Ein Erwachsener kann dir bestimmt helfen.

Lösung

three (3) dogs

two (2) cats

four (4) cows

one (1) pig

five (5) sheep

Holidays

Ordne diese besonderen Tag in der Reihenfolge, in der sie im Jahr stattfinden. Wenn du weißt, wann sie genau stattfinden, kannst du das Datum dazuschreiben.

Easter

Valentine's Day

Christmas

Halloween

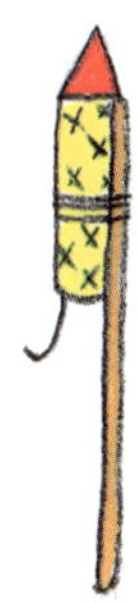

New Year's Eve

1. Valentines Day
2. Halloween
3. Easter
4. Christmas
5. New Years Eve

Lösung

1. Valentine's Day (14th February)
2. Easter (March or April)
3. Halloween (31st October)
4. Christmas (25th December)
5. New Year's Eve (31st December)

Food and drink

Verbinde die englischen Wörter jeweils mit dem richtigen Bild.

Lösung

milk
muffin
bread
banana
coffee
egg
cheese
apples
muesli
water
orange juice
ham

At the table

Zum Essen und Trinken braucht man Geschirr und Besteck.
Ergänze die Sätze mit den richtigen Utensilien.

1. I eat muesli with a ___spoon___.

2. I drink hot chocolate in a ______________.

3. I eat spaghetti with a ______________.

4. I cut bread with a ______________.

5. I drink water in a ______________.

6. I eat a sandwich on a ______________.

Lösung

1. spoon
2. cup
3. fork
4. knife
5. glass
6. plate

Find the words

Kreuze an, welche Wörter du schon auf Englisch sagen kannst.

Nun schau, ob du die acht Wörter im Raster findest.
Die Wörter sind alle vorwärts zu lesen – entweder waagerecht →, senkrecht ↓ oder diagonal ↘. Male einen Kringel um jedes Wort, das du findest.

A	C	V	I	N	H	C	X	B	E
K	B	A	N	A	N	A	Y	M	L
W	R	J	L	S	I	R	M	Z	C
G	E	H	F	A	B	Q	K	T	H
N	A	F	A	P	P	L	E	O	E
U	D	R	Z	F	D	D	T	Q	E
M	O	X	M	U	F	F	I	N	S
O	I	L	T	X	R	Y	W	A	E
W	W	L	S	Q	J	H	O	G	C
J	Q	O	K	F	W	A	T	E	R

Lösung

A	C	V	I	N	H	C	X	B	E
K	B	A	N	A	N	A	Y	M	L
W	R	J	L	S	I	R	M	Z	C
G	E	H	F	A	B	Q	K	T	H
N	A	F	A	P	P	L	E	O	E
U	D	R	Z	F	D	D	T	Q	E
M	O	X	M	U	F	F	I	N	S
O	I	L	T	X	R	Y	W	A	E
W	W	L	S	Q	J	H	O	G	C
J	Q	O	K	F	W	A	T	E	R

Lucy's house

Lucy beschreibt Fred ihr Haus. Male ein Bild davon.

Lösung

Das **Haus** hat eine blaue Tür, grüne Fenster, ein rotes Dach und einen Kamin. Es hat fünf Fenster und einen Garten mit Bäumen und Blumen.

The right clothes

Es ist Dezember und draußen ist es sehr kalt, **very cold**. Lucy und Fred wollen in den Weihnachtsferien verreisen, können sich aber nicht einigen, wohin. Fred möchte gerne Ski fahren aber Lucy möchte lieber dorthin, wo es auch im Winter warm und sonnig, **warm and sunny,** ist. Wer packt was in seinen eigenen Koffer? Schreibe die richtigen Wörter in die Koffer.

Lösung

Lucy nimmt mit: sandals, swimsuit, shorts, sunglasses, T-Shirt, sun hat

Fred nimmt mit: pullover, trousers, coat, scarf, gloves, boots

The body

Wie heißen die Körperteile?

Lösung

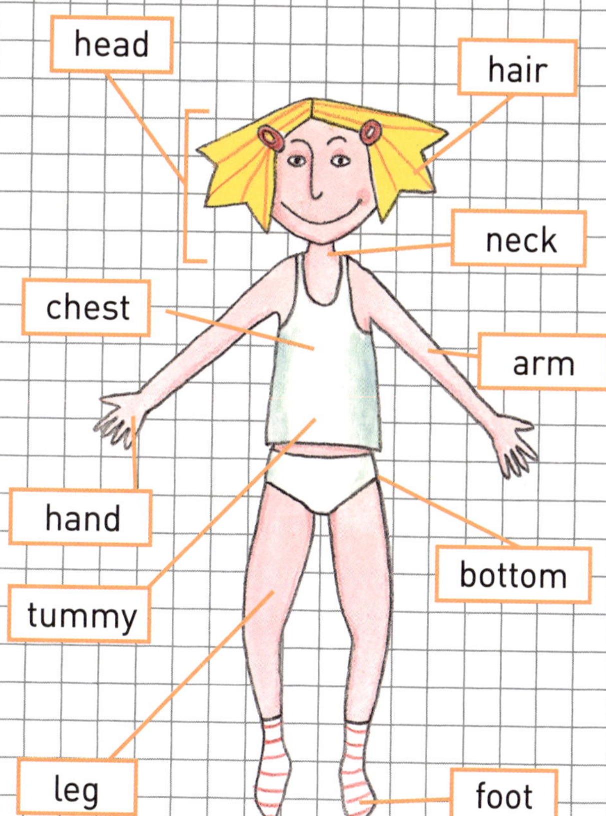

Where are they?

In dem Raster sind die englischen Wörter für die folgenden Körperteile versteckt. Findest du sie? Die Wörter sind alle vorwärts zu lesen – entweder waagerecht →, senkrecht ↓ oder diagonal ↘.

Kopf Po Hand Mund Bein Arm Finger Augen Hals Bauch

W	H	X	C	V	M	R	L	A	B
E	A	I	Y	L	O	E	Q	E	J
R	N	R	P	F	U	U	B	J	G
T	D	T	M	V	T	Z	O	I	F
U	F	S	E	U	H	O	T	M	H
M	G	E	P	F	C	V	T	S	D
M	K	H	E	A	D	M	O	A	N
Y	E	J	S	I	B	Y	M	X	E
A	S	H	E	Y	E	S	R	W	C
F	I	N	G	E	R	K	S	A	K

Lösung

W	H	X	C	V	M	R	L	A	B
E	A	I	Y	L	O	E	Q	E	J
R	N	R	P	F	U	U	B	J	G
T	D	T	M	V	T	Z	O	I	F
U	F	S	E	U	H	O	T	M	H
M	G	E	P	F	C	V	T	S	D
M	K	H	E	A	D	M	O	A	N
Y	E	J	S	I	B	Y	M	X	E
A	S	H	E	Y	E	S	R	W	C
F	I	N	G	E	R	K	S	A	K

Where?

Schau dir die Bilder an und vervollständige anschließend die Sätze. Ergänze jeweils die richtige Präposition, das heißt das richtige Verhältniswort.

1. Fips is ________ the bed.

2. Lucy is ________ the bed.

3. The books are ________ the shelf.

4. The clock is ________ the shelf.

5. Lucy is sitting ________ the armchair.

6. The armchair is ________ the window.

7. The picture is ________ the suitcase.

8. The chair is ________ the suitcase.

Tipp: Die Wörter, die Fips dir zeigt, helfen dir, die Sätze zu verstehen.

Lösung

1. in
2. next to
3. on
4. under
5. in
6. in front of
7. behind
8. next to

Fruit and vegetables

Kreuze an, welche Wörter du bereits auf Englisch kennst und schreibe die Namen der **fruit and vegetables**, des Obst und Gemüses, auf die Linien.

1. ________________

2. ________________

3. ________________

4. ________________

5. ________________

6. ________________

7. ________________

8. ________________

9. ________________

10. ________________

11. ________________

12. ________________

Lösung

1. Banane – banana
2. Kirsche – cherry
3. Apfel – apple
4. Kürbis – pumpkin
5. Orange – orange
6. Gurke – cucumber
7. Birne – pear
8. Zitrone – lemon
9. Tomate – tomato
10. Blaubeeren – blueberries
11. Karotte – carrot
12. Erdbeere – strawberry

Odd one out

In jeder Reihe passt immer ein Wort nicht. Welches?
Streiche es durch.

banana - apple - orange juice - strawberry

carrot - cucumber - pumpkin - bread

carrot - cake - muffin - chocolate

orange juice - tomato - water - milk

knife - fork - spoon - chocolate

cup - plate - cake - glass

spaghetti - breakfast - lunch - dinner

bread - cake - muffin - tomato

to read - to eat - to drink - to cook

Wenn du ausdrücken möchtest, dass dir etwas schmeckt, kannst du sagen:
Mm, this tastes good.
oder **I like this.**
oder auch **Yummy!**

Lösung

orange juice

bread

carrot

tomato

chocolate

cake

spaghetti

tomato

to read

Which house?

Welche Beschreibung passt zu welchem Haus? Verbinde.

1. ☐
This house has a garden.
It has two windows.

2. ☐
This house is very small.
It has a green door.

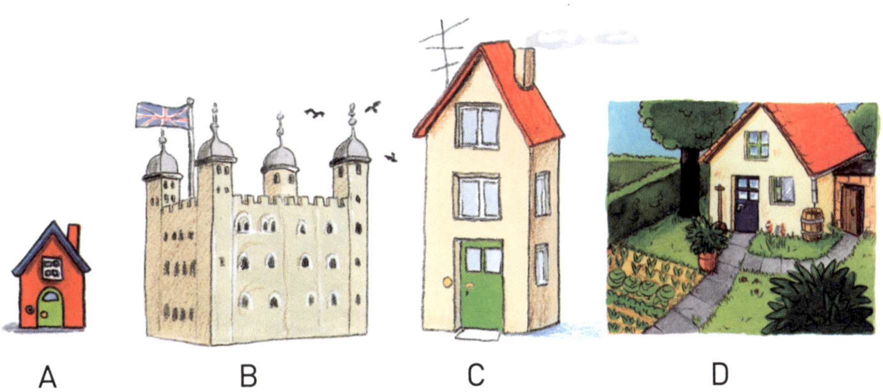

3. ☐
This house is very big.
It has lots of windows.
The Queen of England
lives in this house.

4. ☐
This house is very tall.
It has four windows and
a green door.

Lösung

1. D
2. A
3. B
4. C

What's the weather like?

Kannst du jedem Satz das passende Bild zuordnen?

1. The sun is shining. ◯
2. It's raining. ◯
3. It's foggy. ◯
4. It's snowing. ◯
5. It's windy. ◯
6. There's a storm. ◯

What's the weather like? Und wie ist das Wetter bei dir heute? Schreibe hier auf Englisch hin, wie das Wetter ist.

Lösung

1. D
2. A
3. F
4. B
5. E
6. C

Around the year

Im Herbst gehen Lucy und Fips gerne spazieren und sammeln bunte Blätter oder lassen ihren Drachen, **their kite**, steigen. Sie überlegen, was sie am nächsten Tag machen werden und malen davon ein Bild. Wenn du die Flächen so anmalst, wie angegeben, wirst du sehen, was sie vorhaben!

1 **red**	3 **green**	5 **orange**	7 **black**	9 **pink**
2 **blue**	4 **yellow**	6 **brown**	8 **white**	10 **purple**

Lösung

Antwort

Animals on a farm

Schreibe die englischen Namen der animals, also der Tiere, unten auf die Linien.

Lösung

sheep, hen, chick, pig, cow, goat, mouse, horse, cat

School words

In dem Bleistift sind die Namen von fünf Gegenständen versteckt. Male einen Kringel um jedes Wort herum.

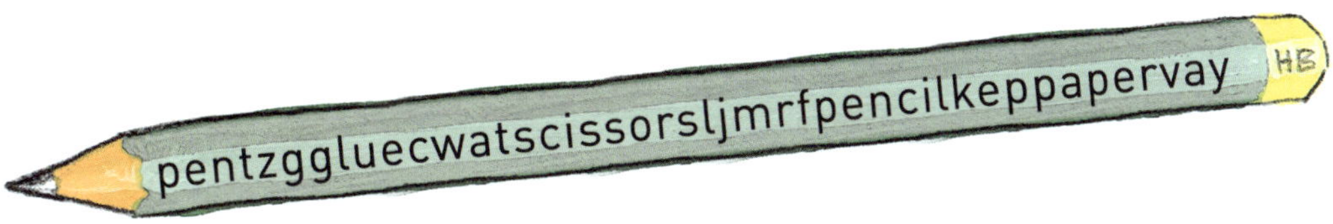

My schoolbag

Schreibe hier fünf Gegenstände auf, die sich in deinem Schulranzen, **in your schoolbag**, befinden.

____

____

____

____

____

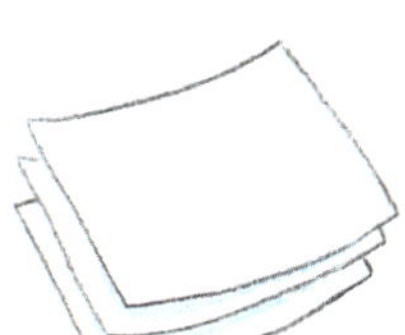

Lösung

pen tzg **glue** cwat **scissors** ljmrf **pencil** kep **paper** vay

pen Füller

glue Klebstoff

scissors Schere

pencil Stift

paper Papier

Missing

A. Oops, wer hat hier Buchstaben geklaut? In jedem Wort fehlt ein Buchstabe. Ergänze die fehlenden Buchstaben, damit die Wörter wieder richtig geschrieben sind.

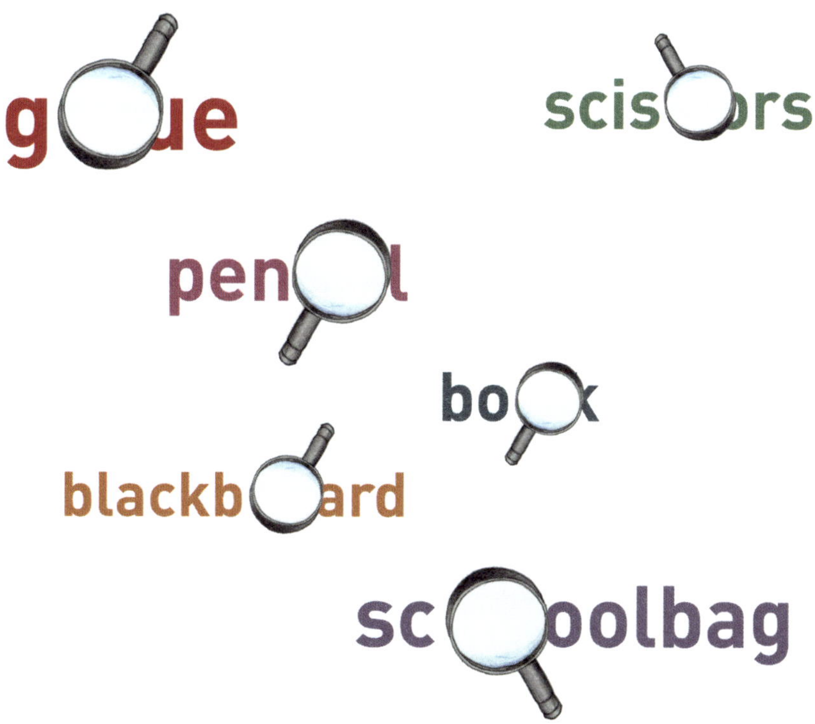

B. Mit den fehlenden Buchstaben kannst du außerdem diesen Satz vervollständigen. Sortiere sie in die richtige Reihenfolge und finde das Lösungswort:

Lucy and Fred are at ____________________.

Lösung

A. glue, scissors, pencil, book, blackboard, schoolbag

B. Lucy and Fred are at **school**.

Free time

Fred, Lucy und Fips sind in ihrer Freizeit immer sehr beschäftigt!
Verbinde jeden Satz jeweils mit dem passenden Bild.

A 

B 

1. Lucy is **swimming**.
2. Fred is **cycling**.
3. Lucy is **painting**.
4. Fips is **reading**.
5. Fred is **playing football**.
6. Lucy is **singing**.
7. Fips is **eating**.
8. Fred and Fips are **playing a game**.

C 

D 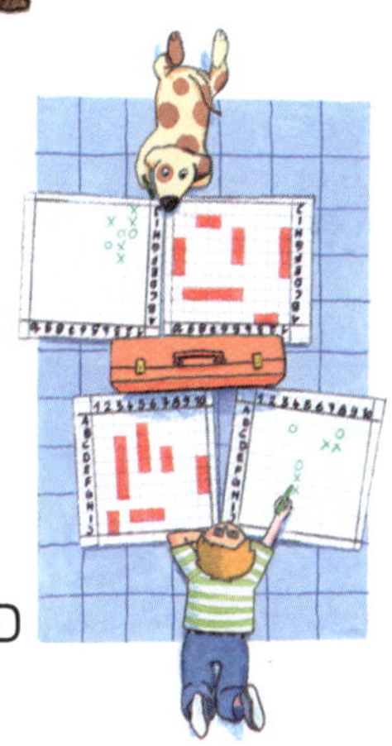

E 

F 

G 

H 

Lösung

1. A
2. F
3. H
4. B
5. E
6. G
7. C
8. D

I like ...

Was machst du gerne in deiner Freizeit? Liste die Sachen, die du gerne machst, unten in der Tabelle in der Spalte **I like ...** auf und die, die du nicht magst, in der Spalte **I don't like ...** auf. Hier findest du schon mal ein paar Vorschläge:

playing football **reading** **doing homework** **swimming** **cycling** **dancing** **listening to music** **eating ice-cream** **singing** **walking** **riding** **watching TV** **cooking** **playing a game** **painting** **playing tennis** **writing**

I like ...	I don't like ...

Lösung

homework – die Hausaufgaben
listening to music – Musik hören
watching TV – fernsehen
writing – schreiben

Who sits where?

Das sind Schüler der Klasse 3b. Alle Kinder hören aufmerksam zu, während der Lehrer, Mr Black, etwas erklärt. Alle Kinder bis auf eines ... Finde heraus, wer sich von Fips ablenken lässt. Lies dir den Text genau durch und schreibe die Namen der Kinder unter die Schreibtische.

Ella sits next to Lucy. Sophie sits behind Ella. Sophie sits between Tom and Maxi. Philipp sits in front of Maxi.

Lösung

Tom	Sophie	Maxi
Lucy	Ella	Philipp

Please listen, **Maxi**!

Ship ahoy!

Willst du auch wie Lucy ein **raft** (Floß) basteln?
Das geht ganz einfach! Dann heißt es **ship ahoy**!

You need:

16 corks (Korken)

1 thin twig (ein dünner Ast)

paper

crayons

glue (Klebstoff)

modelling clay (Knete)

Lösung

Noch ein Tipp, damit du in der Anleitung alles verstehst: **row** heißt Reihe und **holes** sind Löcher.

My Bike

Beantworte die folgenden Fragen.

1. I have got a bike. ☐ yes ☐ no
2. My bike is ________________ (z.B. **red**, **blue** ...).
3. This is my bike:

4. I like cycling. ☐ yes ☐ no
5. I go to school on my bike. ☐ yes ☐ no
6. My family has _______ bikes.

Lösung

Wichtige **Fahrradwörter** sind außerdem:

to ride a bike mit dem Fahrrad fahren

bike lane Fahrradweg

mountain bike Mountainbike

racing bike Rennrad

What is it?

A. Kreuze an, welche Wörter du bereits auf Englisch kennst.

1. ________________

2. ________________

3. ________________

4. ________________

5. ________________

6. ________________

7. ________________

8. ________________

9. ________________

B. Wähle zu jedem Bild jeweils das richtige Wort und schreibe es auf die Linie.

bird **tree** **leaf** **butterfly** **worm**

caterpillar **grass** **flower** **bee**

Lösung

1. tree
2. flower
3. caterpillar
4. leaf
5. bird
6. grass
7. bee
8. worm
9. butterfly

Which animal?

A. Fips riecht etwas Interessantes.
Schreibe die englischen Wörter in die Kästchen.

					1			

		2		

3		

4			

						5				

6			

B. Einige Buchstaben sind nummeriert. Schreibe sie in das Lösungsfeld und du findest heraus, welches Tier Fips entdeckt hat.

1	2	3	4	5	6

C. Auf Deutsch heißt es: ______________________________

Lösung

A. Von oben: butterfly, grass, bee, bird, caterpillar, tree

B. rabbit

C. Kaninchen

Lots of animals

Verbinde die Wörter mit den passenden Bildern.

elephant tiger lion
bear
sheep

dog bird
pig cow
spider

Lösung

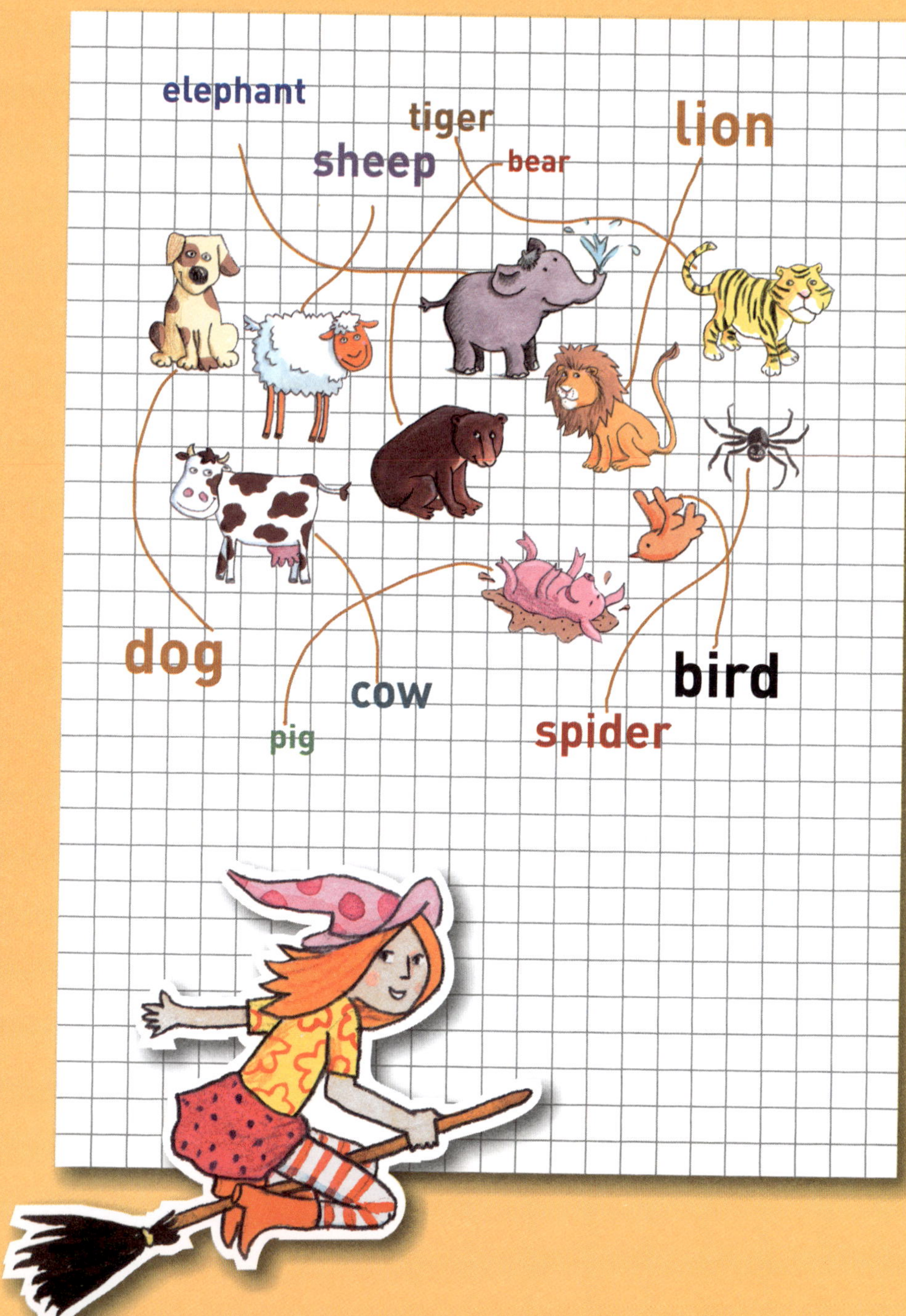

One dog – two dogs

Alle Wörter stehen in der Einzahl. Schreibe hier die Mehrzahl auf.

one dog	– two __________	one elephant	– two __________
one sheep	– two __________	one lion	– two __________
one tiger	– two __________	one cow	– two __________
one bear	– two __________	one pig	– two __________
one bird	– two __________	one spider	– two __________

Who is it?

Welche Tiere werden hier beschrieben?

1. This animal is brown and white. It gives milk.
   It's a ________________.
2. This animal is grey. It is very big and very heavy.
   It's an ________________.
3. This animal has wings.
   It's a ________________.
4. This animal is brown. It has a long tail and a mane.
   It's a ________________.
5. This animal is pink. It likes mud.
   It's a ________________.
6. This animal is very small.
   It has eight legs.
   It's a ________________.

to give – geben
wings – die Flügel
tail – der Schwanz
mane – die Mähne
mud – der Schlamm

Lösung

dogs, elephants, sheep, lions, tigers, cows, bears, pigs, birds, spiders

1. cow

2. elephant

3. bird

4. lion

5. pig

6. spider

At the market

Lucy ist mit ihrem Papa auf dem Markt und kauft **fruit and vegetables**, Obst und Gemüse, ein. Vervollständige das Gespräch zwischen Lucy und dem Obsthändler. Wähle die passenden Sätze aus.

Lucy: ______________________________

Obsthändler: Hello! Can I help you?

Lucy: ______________________________

Obsthändler: Here you are. Ten apples.

Lucy: ______________________________

Obsthändler: Here you are. Five bananas.

Lucy: ______________________________

Obsthändler: It's one pound seventy.

Lucy: ______________________________

Obsthändler: Thank you. Bye!

1. And five bananas, please.
2. Hello!
3. Here you are. One pound seventy.
4. I'd like ten apples, please.
5. Thank you! How much does it cost?

Lösung

2, 4, 1, 5, 3

A trip to London

Vervollständige die Geschichte. Trage neben jedem Bild das richtige englische Wort ein.

Fred is going to London. He waits for the  ______.

He gets off at the station. He buys a ticket with some 

________. The  ________ arrives. Fred gets on the

train. The train leaves at  ________________.

The train arrives in London at  ________________.

In London there are lots of  ________.

Fred waits at the  ________ ________. When the light

is  ________Fred crosses the  ________.

He wants to visit Buckingham Palace. He catches

the  ________.

Lösung

Fred is going to London. He waits for the **tram**. He gets off at the station. He buys a ticket with some **money**. The **train** arrives. Fred gets on the train. The train leaves at **ten o'clock**. The train arrives in London at **half past twelve**. In London there are lots of **cars**. Fred waits at the **traffic light**. When the light is **green** Fred crosses the **road**. He wants to visit Buckingham Palace. He catches the **bus**.

What's Lucy doing?

Schau dir die Bilder an und entscheide, welche Antwort richtig ist.

1. Lucy is

- ☐ going on holiday.
- ☐ reading a book.
- ☐ eating an ice-cream.

2. Lucy is

- ☐ in the mountains.
- ☐ at the beach.
- ☐ at school.

3. Lucy is wearing

- ☐ a blue swimsuit.
- ☐ a green bikini.
- ☐ a yellow T-shirt.

4. Lucy is

- ☐ playing a game.
- ☐ riding a bike.
- ☐ swimming.

5. Fips is lying

- ☐ on the deckchair.
- ☐ next to the deckchair.
- ☐ under the deckchair.

6. Lucy is playing with

- ☐ three children.
- ☐ five children.
- ☐ eight children.

Lösung

1. going on holiday
2. at the beach
3. a green bikini
4. swimming
5. under the deckchair
6. five children

Postcards

Lucy ist im Urlaub. Sie schreibt Postkarten und Briefe an ihre Freundinnen.

Das kannst auch du machen! Lucy war ganz schlau und hat sich einen Brief für fast alle Gelegenheiten vorgeschrieben. **Good idea!** Gute Idee! Außerdem hat sie noch ein paar Vorschläge gemacht, was du sonst schreiben könntest.

Hi ____________,

How are you? I'm fine. I'm on holidays in ____________.
The weather is (1) ____________.
(2) ____________.
I (3) ____________ the food here. My favourite dish is ____________. We have visited (4) ____________ places.
We went to ____________.
I'm having a (5) ____________ time here.
I don't miss school at all, but I miss you.
See you soon,
bye,
____________.

Lösung

(1) fine / soso / awful

(2) It's raining / It's cloudy / The sun is shining

(3) like / don't like / hate

(4) lots of / a few / very few

(5) great / boring / horrible

Wenn du deinen Freunden aus dem Urlaub schreiben möchtest, wirst du folgende Dinge benötigen:

postcards – Postkarten oder
writing paper – Briefpapier
envelopes – Briefumschläge
stamps – Briefmarken
address book – Adressbuch

My school

Trage ein.

1. My school is: ______________________________

2. My teacher's name is: ______________________________

3. My class is: ______________________________

4. I go to school at: ______________________________ 

5. I come home at: ______________________________ 

6. My favourite subjects are: ______________________________

7. I sit next to: ______________________________

8. I go school:

- ☐ on foot
- ☐ by bike
- ☐ by bus
- ☐ by car
- ☐ by tram

Lösung

Hier schreibst du deinen persönlichen **Schulsteckbrief**. Zeige ihn doch mal deinem Englischlehrer.

Find the school words

In dem Raster sind die englischen Übersetzungen von den folgenden zehn Wörtern, die mit Schule zu tun haben, versteckt. Findest du sie alle? Die Wörter sind vorwärts zu lesen – entweder waagerecht →, senkrecht ↓ oder diagonal ↘.

Stift Lehrer Kleber Bleistift Tafel
Klasse Schule Fach Schulbuch Schere

S	A	S	C	H	O	O	L	B	O	O	K
P	C	L	H	L	Z	R	U	I	Y	Q	B
R	I	H	E	R	A	F	B	N	A	S	A
P	K	C	O	G	C	S	J	G	L	U	E
E	W	P	Q	O	A	V	S	L	T	B	I
N	X	E	S	K	L	R	B	T	A	J	O
C	U	N	V	X	B	Q	S	E	L	E	R
I	V	G	A	B	W	T	Y	A	R	C	Z
L	L	H	W	E	X	U	K	C	I	T	G
S	C	I	S	S	O	R	S	H	F	H	A
F	G	H	T	Z	U	I	B	E	K	L	J
B	L	A	C	K	B	O	A	R	D	Y	O

Lösung

S	A	S	C	H	O	O	L	B	O	O	K
P	C	L	H	L	Z	R	U	I	Y	Q	B
R	I	H	E	R	A	F	B	N	A	S	A
P	K	C	O	G	C	S	J	G	L	U	E
E	W	P	Q	O	A	V	S	L	T	B	I
N	X	E	S	K	L	R	B	T	A	J	O
C	U	N	V	X	B	Q	S	E	L	E	R
I	V	G	A	B	W	T	Y	A	R	C	Z
L	L	H	W	E	X	U	K	C	I	T	G
S	C	I	S	S	O	R	S	H	F	H	A
F	G	H	T	Z	U	I	B	E	K	L	J
B	L	A	C	K	B	O	A	R	D	Y	O

Counting fish

Ui, im Meer wimmelt es ja nur so von Fischen! Wie viele Fische entdeckt Fips beim Tauchen? Zähle sie auf Englisch!

◯ red fish ◯ green fish ◯ yellow fish

◯ pink fish ◯ blue fish

Außerdem schwimmt im Meer:

◯ brown dog

Lösung

five red fish

one green fish

eight yellow fish

twelve pink fish

three blue fish

one brown dog

Around the year

A. Kreuze die Jahreszeiten an, die du auf Englisch schon benennen kannst.

☐

☐

☐

☐

B. Zu welcher Jahreszeit gehören diese Dinge? Verbinde die Bilder jeweils mit der richtigen Jahreszeit.

Lösung

A. winter, spring, summer, autumn

B.

The months

In diesem Kreis stehen die Monatsnamen. Trenne die Monatsnamen jeweils mit einem Strich. Zieh den Strich von der Mitte bis zum Rand und teile so den Kreis in 12 Stücke auf, wie bei einem Kuchen! Male anschließend deinen Jahreskuchen an – jeden Monat in einer passenden Farbe.

The seasons

Zu welcher Jahreszeit gehören die Monate? Male die Kästchen jeweils in der richtigen Farbe an.

spring summer autumn winter

August December January November June May April October February July March September

Lösung

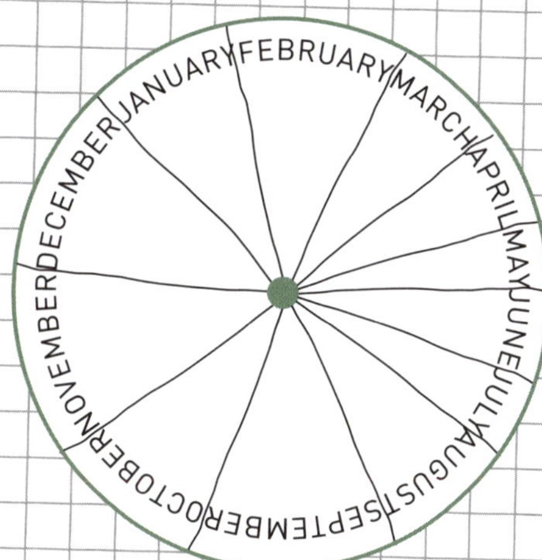

spring:	March, April, May
summer:	June, July, August
autumn:	September, October, November
winter:	December, January, February

The days of the week

A. Ui, die gefräßige Schlange hat die Wochentage verschlungen! Findest du alle sieben Tage? Male einen Kringel um jedes Wort.

B. In der Schlange sollten nun sieben Buchstaben übrig bleiben. Sie ergeben das englische Wort für Wochenende. Es heißt:

____

C. Schreibe hier die Wochentage in der richtigen Reihenfolge auf Englisch auf:

1. ____________________
2. ____________________
3. ____________________
4. ____________________
5. ____________________
6. ____________________
7. ____________________

Lösung

A. MONDAY W TUESDAY EE WEDNESDAY K THURSDAY E FRIDAY N SATURDAY D SUNDAY

B. weekend

C.
1. Monday
2. Tuesday
3. Wednesday
4. Thursday
5. Friday
6. Saturday
7. Sunday

When?

Lies den folgenden Text in Ruhe durch. Entscheide dann, ob die Sätze unten richtig oder falsch sind.

Fred gets up at seven o'clock. He goes to school at quarter to eight. He has lunch at half past twelve. Fred comes home at three o'clock in the afternoon. He plays football at four o'clock. Fred has dinner at six o'clock. He goes to bed at half past eight. Good night!

	richtig	falsch
1. Fred steht um sieben Uhr auf.	☐	☐
2. Er geht um Viertel vor acht zur Schule.	☐	☐
3. Er isst um halb zwölf zu Mittag.	☐	☐
4. Fred kommt vormittags nach Hause.	☐	☐
5. Er spielt um vier Uhr Fußball.	☐	☐
6. Er isst um halb sieben zu Abend.	☐	☐
7. Fred geht um halb neun ins Bett.	☐	☐

Lösung

Richtig: 1, 2, 5 und 7

Falsch: 3, 4 und 6

My day

Jetzt bist du dran! Wie sieht dein Tag aus? Trage die Uhrzeiten ein und vervollständige die Sätze.

I get up at ______________________________

I go to school at ______________________________

I have lunch at ______________________________

I do my homework at ______________________________

I play with my friends at ______________________________

I go to bed at ______________________________

Viertel vor …, Viertel nach … und halb … drückst du auf Englisch so aus:

quarter to three – Viertel vor drei
quarter past three – Viertel nach drei
half past three – halb vier

Aufgepasst! Im Englischen bezieht sich **half past** auf die Stunde, die seit 30 Minuten vorbei ist!

Lösung

Magst du auch noch einen Tagesplan auf Englisch für Samstag oder Sonntag machen?

Numbers

Male die Kästchen jeweils in der richtigen Farbe an.

forty-five

ninety-three

18

61

sixty-one

20

79

fifty-seven

thirty-two

seventy-nine

32

45

84

eighty-four

twenty

sixty-six

93

66

eighteen

57

Lösung

Antwort

84	66	18	79	93
32	57	20	45	61

How much does it cost?

Sicher weißt du schon, dass man in England nicht mit Euro zahlt, sondern mit **pounds** (Pfund) und **pence** (Pence). So sehen die Münzen in England aus:

1p 2p 5p 10p 20p 50p £1

So wie es das Zeichen **€** für Euro gibt, verwendet man in England **£** für Pfund und **p** für Pence. Wenn etwas ein Pfund und zehn Pence kostet, dann schreibt man es **£1.10**. Kostet etwas 50 Pence, schreibt man es **50p**.

Verbinde die Münzen jeweils mit dem richtigen Preisschild.

1. 

2. 

3. 

4. 

5. 

Lösung

1. bread
2. milk
3. muffin
4. hamburger
5. apples

Bitte hier ausfüllen

und in der nächstgelegenen Schülerhilfe vor Ort abgeben.
Weitere Infos über die Schülerhilfe unter www.schuelerhilfe.de.

Vorname

Name

PLZ

Ort

Straße

Geburtsdatum

Telefon

E-Mail

*Gültig nur in teilnehmenden Schülerhilfen. Gültig nur für Neukunden. Nur ein Gutschein pro Kunde. Nicht gültig in Verbindung mit anderen Aktionen, Angeboten, Coupons oder Rabatten. Gültig nur für Einzelunterricht in kleinen Gruppen.